IF I WERE A MAN AND HAD A WIFE

Brenda B. Matthews

BEA-MOR Publishing

Copyright © 2006 Brenda B. Matthews

All rights reserved.

No part of this book may be reproduced, or stored in a retrieval system, or transmitted in any form or by any means, electronic, mechanical, photocopying, recording, or otherwise, without express written permission of the publisher.

Email: brendabmatthews@att.net
All scriptures are taken from the King James Version of the Bible.

Bea-Mor Publishing
Second Edition 2020

ISBN 13: 978-0-9891368-6-0
ISBN 10: 0989136868

Printed in the United States of America

Editors
Minister Josephine Johnson
Sister Regina Ware
First Lady Denise Battle
Dr. Cassandra Crittenden

DEDICATION

I dedicate this book to the husbands who live according to God's Word in their marriage, the rearing of their children, including step-children; and standing as the head of their home, as Jesus is the head of the church. Thanks for being that Family Man God designed you to be! You shall receive a great reward!

To the husbands who live "not" according to God's Word, know that it is not too late to change. It is not too late to repent. It is not too late to tell God you're sorry for abiding "not" by His Word. It is not too late to ask God for forgiveness. It is not too late to apologize to your wife for your great mess ups. It is not too late to ask her to forgive you. It is not too late to begin again. The thief who hung on the cross next to Jesus began his life again with Jesus in paradise, And Jesus said unto him, Verily I say unto thee, To day shalt thou be with me in paradise, Luke 23:43. The key word is TODAY! Your life can change TODAY! What a Promise!

TO ALL GOD'S CHILDREN

My prayer is that your heart is touched, your spirit is moved, and your mind is changed while reading and upon reading my book. It displays how a wife is to be treated by her husband according to the Word of God. It also displays how a husband is to treat his wife according to the Word of God. It was written just for you!

Chapter One

If I Were A Man And Had A Wife

Chapter Two

Long Before Marriage

Chapter Three

The Christian Family Man

Chapter Four

The Christian Man With A Family

Chapter Five

The Ungodly Family Man

Chapter Six

The Ungodly Man With A Family

Chapter Seven

The Wicked Family Man

Chapter Eight

The Wicked Man With A Family

Chapter Nine

The Family Man vs. The Man With The Family

Chapter Ten

The Leader

Chapter Eleven

3 Steps To The Plan Of Salvation

Chapter Twelve

A Note To The Women

DEDICATION

I dedicate this book to the husbands who live according to God's Word in their marriage, the rearing of their children, including step children; and standing as the head of their home, as Jesus is the head of the church. Thanks for being that Family Man God designed you to be! You shall receive a great reward!

To the husbands who live "not" according to God's Word, know that it is not too late to change. It is not too late to repent. It is not too late to tell God you're sorry for abiding "not" by His Word. It is not too late to ask God for forgiveness. It is not too late to apologize to your wife for your great mess ups. It is not too late to ask her to forgive you. It is not too late to begin again. The thief who hung on the cross next to Jesus began his life again with Jesus in paradise, **And Jesus said unto him, Verily I say unto thee, To day shalt thou be with me in paradise, Luke 23:43.** The key word is TODAY! Your life can change TODAY! What a Promise!

Chapter One

IF I WERE A MAN AND HAD A WIFE!

Because of my reverence unto the Lord, I fear His wrath, I fear His consequences of sin, I fear burning in Hell eternally, I fear His chastening, I fear unforgiveness, I fear not repenting, I fear walking in the imagination of my own heart; therefore, my prayer is that the heart of husbands and aspiring husbands is touched and changed today so that his marriage will be in line with God's will. Husbands, when your marriage is in accordance with God's Word, nothing can separate the two of you, not an ex, not a lie, not a child, not money, not possessions, not education, not a friend, not an in-law, and not temptation.

When your marriage is in God's hand, He will direct you and if you follow His pathway of righteousness, you cannot slip. If you keep your eyes on Jesus, you will walk on the waters whether the waters are high, calm, wavy, or roaring. Husbands, put all of your faith, trust, and hope in the Lord. Pray without ceasing and pray together. Get to know your wife, learn what God has blessed you with internally, not just externally. Protect your wife and let no man disrespect her. Listen to her with an open mind and respond to her verbally, not silently; it's okay to use her suggestions; it's okay to praise her and thank her; it's okay to give her credit; it's okay to love her, publishing with a loud voice to others that you love her. Take a moment out of your busy schedule to call her just to say hello or just to see how her day is going. Send her cards, flowers, e-mail, or perfume just because; don't wait until Valentine's Day to express love to her; practice daily. Ask God to show you how to excite her; surely He knows, He created her!

If I were a man and had a wife, I would have an interest in every word she speaks; every tear that drops; every nail that breaks; every scratch on her body; every meal she eats; every doctor's visit she has; and every book she reads. I would anxiously come home from work to handle my house business, then my home business, then my husband business. I may come home to my husband business first, then get back to the house and home business later! I would always want to know from her what is it that I could do to make her day better. I would want her to always remember that I am available to her and that other than God, nothing is more important to me.

Remember husbands, take care of your wife; God gave her to you; she's precious, she's yours, she's you!

Chapter Two

LONG BEFORE MARRIAGE

Prior to marriage, I would have researched the origin of the woman from the Bible. When I learned in Genesis 2:18, And the LORD God said, It is not good that the man should be alone; I will make him an help meet for him, I would have realized that God knows my needs as He did Adam's. I would have also realized that He will supply my needs according to His riches in Glory.

Genesis 2:21-23, And the LORD God caused a deep sleep to fall upon Adam, and he slept: and He took one of his ribs, and closed up the flesh instead thereof; And the rib, which the LORD God had taken from man, made he a woman, and brought her unto the man. And Adam said, This is now bone of my bones, and flesh of my flesh: she shall be called Woman, because she was taken out of Man.

Upon reading these verses, I would have thought that if God could form a woman from a man while he was in a deep sleep, what could He form in a woman (his wife) while he's asleep. This means that while man is asleep, it is not known what God is creating in a woman. This also means that after a man marries, he'd better **wake up** out of his deep sleep, once in a while, to see what God may be putting in his wife's spirit!

I must share 14 jewels I would have learned about wives and I pray that they help you:

1. I would have learned that God gave the wife to man which means that wives are gifts from God; Every good gift and every perfect gift is from above, and cometh down from the Father of

lights, with whom is no variableness
(inconsistency), neither shadow of turning (when the moon turns, there's a shadow but even in the shadow, God changes not), James 1:17.

2. I would have learned that wives become bone of her husbands' bones and flesh of her husbands' flesh. They become one! Therefore shall a man leave his father and his mother, and shall cleave unto his wife: and they shall be one flesh, Genesis 2:24.

When two becomes one, and God brought the two together, I would have learned a few things here:

    a. If one is hurt, so is the other.
    b. If one is down, so is the other.
    c. If one is low on money, so is the other.
    d. If one is happy, so is the other.
    e. If one is renown, so is the other.
    f. If one has troubles, so does the other.
    g. If one is hungry, so is the other.
    h. If one is in need, so is the other.
    i. If one is present, so is the other.
    j. If one is a grandparent, so is the other.
    k. If one has credit, so does the other.

3. I would have learned that God created marriage to complete couples; the husband's responsibility is to love his wife as he loves himself; and wives are "help meets" and she is to help her husband in areas in which he lacks.

4. I would have learned that when God ordain marriages, anyone who interferes in any way, intentionally or unintentionally, shall suffer consequences from God.

5. I would have learned that if the husband or wife allows others to interfere with their marriage, in any way, there is a reaping process. All parties involved shall reap!

6. I would have learned that husbands and wives are to be

open, honest, and not ashamed while with each other in every thing ranging from childhood hurts, to the death of loved ones. And they were both naked, the man and his wife, and were not ashamed, Genesis 2:25.

7. I would have learned that women are precious, so precious that God equated them to wisdom and I would have written down scriptures, cut them out, and placed them on my refrigerator, to constantly remind me of the greatness of women and the greatness in women!

Proverbs 2:1-5
My son, if thou wilt receive my words, and hide my commandments with thee; So that thou incline thine ear unto wisdom, and apply thine heart to understanding;

Yea, if thou criest after knowledge, and liftest up thy voice for understanding;

If thou seekest **her** as silver, and searchest for **her** as for hid treasures;

Then shalt thou understand the fear of the LORD, and find the knowledge of God.

Proverbs 3:13-18
Happy is the man that findeth wisdom, and the man that getteth understanding.

For the merchandise of it is better than the merchandise of silver, and the gain thereof than fine gold.
She is more precious than rubies: and all the things thou canst desire are not to be compared unto **her**.

Length of days is in **her** right hand; and in **her** left hand riches and honour.

Her ways are ways of pleasantness, and all **her** paths are peace.

She is a tree of life to them that lay hold upon **her**: and happy is every one that retaineth **her**.

Proverbs 4:5-9

Get wisdom, get understanding: forget it not; neither decline from the words of my mouth.

Forsake **her** not, and **she** shall preserve thee: love **her**, and **she** shall keep thee.

Wisdom is the principal thing; therefore get wisdom: and with all thy getting get understanding.

Exalt **her**, and **she** shall promote thee: **she** shall bring thee to honour, when thou dost embrace **her**.

She shall give to thine head an ornament of grace: a crown of glory shall **she** deliver to thee.

GOD EQUATES
(God Fearing Women)
TO WISDOM

SUMMARY OF SCRIPTURES ABOVE

WIVES	WISDOM
Fragile/Delicate	Fragile/Delicate
Worthy	Worthy
Applies Knowledge	Applied knowledge
Precious	Precious
Preparers/Thinker	Preparation
Priceless/Valuable	Priceless/Valuable
Provider	Provides
Powerful	Power
Preserver	Preserver
Pleasant	Pleasant
Tree of Life	Tree of Life
Crown of Glory	Crown of Glory
Gives Birth	Gives Birth (ministries)
Honorable	Honorable
Full of Peace	Full of Peace
Joyous	Joyous
Riches	Riches

8. I would have learned that WIVES are to be treated as WISDOM is to be treated with:

- CARE
- PROTECTION
- TENDERNESS
- PRAISE
- THANKSGIVING
- APPRECIATION
- RESPECT
- JOY
- KINDNESS
- LOVE

9. I would have learned that the wife is the weaker vessel, I Peter 3:7, and I would have researched "weaker vessel".

A weak vessel defined is a vessel lacking strength.

A weaker vessel defined is a woman with lesser strength than the man.

The weaker vessel does not mean that the woman's mind is weak or weaker; it does not mean that her physical body is weak or weaker; and neither does it mean that the woman is foolish.

The weaker vessel means that the woman's heart is weaker meaning that she is (in most cases) more sensitive, more compassionate, and more compromising.

10. I would have learned that wives are to be submissive to their husband and not inferior to him, **Wives, submit yourselves unto your own husbands, as unto the Lord.** Ephesians 5:22. This verse means that wives are to follow the leading of their husband, as he follows Jesus Christ. If he makes a decision, and you both learn later that it was not the best decision made, the wife is not to belittle him making him feel worst. Men, as leaders, struggle with "being wrong". They don't like to error, they don't like others knowing that they have made an error, they like for their wives to honor them, but when they mess up, they feel worthless. This is why wives have to pray asking God to teach them how to handle their husband when this happens. She must ask God to give her the words to speak to her husband to encourage him and comfort him so that he can always feel like her king. Though he makes the final decisions, this doesn't mean that she is inferior (lower or lesser) to him. Remember, she's the weaker vessel, not the weak vessel. If the husband chooses to let his wife make some decisions, he still made a decision; that decision was permitting her to decide.

11. I would have learned that **the husband is the head of his wife**

as Christ is the head of the church; He is the Saviour of the body Ephesians 5:23. This verse means that the husband is responsible for all of his wife's needs; if she needs counseling, he's her counselor; if she needs money, he's the banker; if she's misdirected, he redirects her; if she's lowly, he's the lifter up of her head; if she gets wet, he's the towel; if she gets dirty, he's the soap; She consults him concerning all matters, even trivial; he honors her and let it be known that God blessed him with her; he let it be known to all that she is under his care. He is the leader, she is the follower, but yet, they walk together side by side; it's a mystery that only God can explain. Jesus has authority over the church; He gave his life for the church. The church represents His body; He's the savior. The husband is to have authority over his wife; he is to treat her as if he is her savior; he is to imitate Jesus and give himself for her; he is to save her from affliction, hurt, danger and make sure that she's comforted daily.

12. I would have learned that husbands are to love their wives as Jesus loves the church, and gave himself, Ephesians 5:25. This verse means that the husband is responsible for all of his wife's needs and desires. He is to see to it that she is happy; comforted, loved, honored, cherished, and nourished everyday, not when he chooses to. He is her provider of her home, clothes, money, food, encouragement, guidance, protection, assurance, and reassurance. If a bullet is aimed at her, he'll stand in front of her. He is to love her so much whereas he'd die for her if necessary, as Jesus died for us and gave Himself. Jesus gave His life for us but He also suffered for us. Jesus cried on Calvary for our sins. Husbands, give yourselves to our wife, suffer for your wife, cry unto the Lord on behalf of your wife; share all of you with her and hold nothing back, share your hurts, concerns, and love. She loves listening to you and she is interested in what you're interested in, though she may not be involved directly, she is still interested. Free your spirit up so that you can receive more from God. If you take care of your wife, she will take care of you and so will God; that's a double blessing!

13. I would have learned that men are to love their wives as their own bodies and when a husband loves his wife, he loves himself; he nourishes and cherishes his own flesh, Ephesians 5:28-29. Husbands, this verse means
that you are to treat your wife as if she is your body. Husbands, you won't take a rod and beat the devil out of yourselves; you don't want bruises. Just as you love your outer beauty, love your wife in the same manner. This verse does not mean to just love your wife's outer beauty either. Listen up husbands, you apply body lotions and creams on yourselves more than your wife; you get manicures and pedicures more than your wife; you're at the hair center more than your wife is and you set your next appointment prior to leaving; you live in the mirror; you exercise regularly, drink plenty of water; eat plenty of vegetables, energy bars and shakes; you get the necessary rest, and more. All of this hard work and money spent is to keep that body looking good and its okay for you to take care of yourself; however, if you did not love your bodies, you wouldn't do it. Well, love your wife in the same manner and God will bless you, your wife, and your family. Even though it may seem as if you're not getting blessed here on earth, just know that you have a great reward coming on the other side and that reward is greater than any reward ever!

14. Also, I would have learned that when God created the most precious "gift" ever, the female, He created WOMAN and WIFE simultaneously; another mystery of God's! Thanks God, a job well done!

Once I researched the origin of woman; searched the scriptures, received revelation of the scriptures, and prayed, I would have asked God for a wife. I would have asked Him to prepare me to be the husband I need to be for my wife and to help me to be the head of my home as He desires and requires.

Being that I'm not a man and being that I am a wife, I listed a few things I probably would have done if I were a man and had a wife!

Of the six categories of men listed below, each husband will find himself under one of them and the wife will find her husband under one as well:

- a. The Christian Family Man
- b. The Christian Man With A Family
- c. The Ungodly Family Man
- d. The Ungodly Man With A Family
- e. The Wicked Family Man
- f. The Wicked Man With A Family

Chapter Three

THE CHRISTIAN FAMILY MAN

THE CHRISTIAN FAMILY MAN puts God first; constantly thinking on the goodness of the Lord. He prays without ceasing; he studies the Word; lives by the Word by praising the Lord, worshipping the Lord, fasting, meditating, consecrating, paying tithes, and spreading the Word; he loves his wife as Jesus loves the church and he loves his children. His family is faithful to their church; they pray together, laugh together, eat together, learn together, and love together. He is giving, compassionate, understanding, and enjoys his life. He is full of wisdom, joy, and encouragement. His children are trained to honor God at a young age; He is concerned about his family's needs and supplies them before supplying his. He's trustworthy, kind, gentle, he walks uprightly before the Lord; his conversations are of righteousness; he is forgiving, and he is always walking in the Spirit of humility. **He shall be like a tree planted by the rivers of water** (he is full of sap; sap is moisture in a tree; he is full of life. Sap is evidence that God lives inside of us; the sap flowing through us is the Holy Ghost and without the Holy Ghost, we are powerless. A tree without sap is powerless. When we're full of sap, we will continuously produce fruit, good fruit, even through tumultuous winds and storms), **that bringeth forth his fruit in his season** (for us to produce fruit, seeds are planted within us. The seeds are the infallible Word of God preached or taught. We must be the good ground in which seeds fall upon. **But he that received seed into the good ground is he that heareth the word, and understandeth it; which also beareth fruit**(beareth - witness to others, spreading God's Word, winning souls to Christ) **and bringeth forth fruit**(receive blessings; knowledge, understanding, revelation, money, property, etc.), **some an hundredfold, some sixty, some thirty**, (prosperity will be 100, 60, or 30 times more than what you have; these increases are not percentages meaning that you won't receive 100, 60, or 30 percent more of what you have, but you'll receive 100, 60, or 30 times more than what you already possess), Matthew 13:23.

And his leaf shall not whither, whatsoever he doeth shall prosper (if he starts a business, it shall prosper, if he starts a ministry, it shall prosper, if he plans a trip, it shall prosper, if he writes songs, they shall prosper), Psalm 1:3. A Family Man Ordained By God.

IT IS PRAYER TIME!

Let us pray that God continues to walk with this husband and assure him that His promises are yea and amen. Let us pray that this husband continues to hear, live, and spread God's Word for there is a great reward at the end. Let us pray that God's hands continue to rest upon the roof of this man's home for peace, protection, provision, love, guidance, and comfort. With the resting of God's hand, satan cannot reside there, he cannot get in. Let us pray that this family is daily strengthened by God and that they remember that all of their strength comes from Him! Let us pray that the husband continues to consult God first in all matters; seek Godly counsel; pray effectually and fervently; fast for insight, partake in Daniel Chapter One fast; praise the Lord in the night and day seasons; worship the Lord in the beauty of holiness; meditate on the promises of the Lord; and consecrate, setting himself apart from every thing for a time, In the Name of Jesus.

Chapter Four

THE CHRISTIAN MAN WITH A FAMILY

THE CHRISTIAN MAN WITH A FAMILY is one who had all of the attributes of the Christian Family Man, but he became selfish, greedy of gain, and prideful. He loves his family, but forgot how to love unconditionally.

He makes people outside of his home believe that he is all for his family; he is similar to the Wicked Man With A Family but he is a believer of Jesus Christ. He is faithful to his church; he pays tithes; and he's active within the church. In pride, satan will trick him into thinking that he's greater than his wife and more important than his children. He feels that the wife is privileged to be a part of his life for without him, he thinks that she would fail. Though the husband is to be reverenced by his wife and he is; though he wants his wife to treat him like a king, and she does; this husband tries his best not to treat her like a queen. They used to walk together with the Lord, but he left her; they used to pray together, speaking to the Lord, but he hushed; and they used to cry together in the presence of the Lord, he dried his own tears. He doesn't pray sincerely as he did, he prays enough to say that he's been in prayer. His prayers are not as effective as they once were and neither is his singing and he wonders why.

With pride, envy and jealousy follows. He tries hard to "make" his light shine forgetting that he is to "let" his light shine by God. He is so busy making sure that the "light" doesn't shine upon his wife, unless he shines it; he doesn't realize that the harder he tries, the dimmer his light becomes. If only this husband would grasp the vision that if his wife is successful, so is he; if his wife is known, so is he, but the beautification of it is, if he is the head of the wife, what ever his wife accomplishes, others will praise him for a great work that he has done with and for his wife, even if he has done nothing but criticized. If her light shines, to other people, the husband was the source because he is the head of her; he trained her, he directed her; he encouraged her; and he had her back even though he may not have done anything. He yearns for attention, acceptance, and approval though he is discreet about it. He degrades others in the household because that boosts his self-worth.

There are many Christian Men With A Family who are ministers, pastors, evangelists, teachers, attorneys, doctors, reporters, etc., who are busy with their careers and ministries whereas they have become stressed, worried, and exhausted trying to balance their work, spouse, and children. He misuses his authority as the head of the family and he sometimes does not realize it.

IT IS PRAYER TIME!

This Christian Man With A Family must be delivered; Let us pray that he reprioritize his life. Let us pray that he ask God to forgive him for all that he's done before God makes a move. Let us pray the scripture; if we confess our sins, he is faithful and just to forgive us our sins, and to cleanse us from all unrighteousness, I John 1:9. Let us remember as we pray that only the Power of God can convict a man, change his heart, and redirect his thoughts and ways. Let's pray that God rests His hand upon this husband speedily, In The Name of Jesus.

Chapter Five

THE UNGODLY FAMILY MAN

THE UNGODLY FAMILY MAN loves his family, and takes care of their needs. He will help with household chores, the kids' homework assignments and projects. He is nice, kind, and gentle. His characteristics are similar to The Christian Family Man's. The difference is Jesus Christ is not in his life. He makes decisions based upon logic, experiences, how his parents raised him, books, statistics, daily news and newspapers, and overheard conversations. He does not mistreat his wife; he respects her, praises her, honors her, and cherishes her. He can be trusted by family and friends. His heart is good and he's genuinely giving and forgiving. He doesn't have a prayer life, no church home, and neither will you hear gospel music playing throughout the home or car. His conversation piece usually consists of the weather, sports, rising prices, yard work, news, news updates, and saving for rainy days.

The ungodly are like the chaff (stiff straw-like particles mixed with grains of wheat, oats or rye that separates from the wheat, oats or rye when blown or thrown; it is a worthless substance that has no strength; chaff needs the wheat but the wheat can stand on its' own because it is solid) **which the wind driveth away. Therefore, the ungodly shall not stand in the judgment, nor sinners in the congregation of the righteous. For the LORD knoweth the way of the righteous: but the way of the ungodly shall perish, Psalm 1:4-6.**

If the ungodly are like chaff, and chaff is moved only when blown or thrown, this means that whatever is blown or thrown upon the ungodly, since the ungodly is like chaff, he's going to move in that direction. It's the wind that makes the chaff move. Therefore, when a wind of hatred blows upon the ungodly (the chaff), the ungodly moves in that direction; when a wind of lust blows upon the ungodly (the chaff), the ungodly moves in that direction; when a wind of gossip blows upon the ungodly (the chaff), the ungodly moves in that direction; when a wind of jealousy blows upon the ungodly (the chaff), the ungodly moves in that direction; when a wind of deception, of any kind blows upon the ungodly (the chaff), the ungodly moves in that direction. One thing about chaff, every time the wind blows, the chaff moves. Chaff has no strength; it's anchored to the wheat until the wind blows.

When the ungodly anchors himself to Jesus, he becomes wheat; he shall stand forever, no matter how strong the wind is, he shall not be moved! Let's pray that the ungodly become Godly. Let us pray that the chaff becomes wheat!

If the Ungodly Family Man is asked, "What church do you attend?" He'll name a church he visited once or twice! He doesn't want his family busy with church and church work. He believes that Sunday is a family day and they are to be spent together.

IT IS PRAYER TIME!

Let us pray that this husband develops a desire to know Jesus Christ. Let us pray that this husband receives revelation of God's goodness and mercy. Let us pray that he learns of God's faithfulness and how He exercises loving kindness towards us. Let us pray that this husband calls upon the name of Jesus now and not wait until he's in a whirlwind of trouble to call upon God just for deliverance for a particular time. Ask the Lord to share with this husband that He will laugh at his calamity (trouble) and mock him as he cries out for temporary help from the Lord. Ask the Lord to remind this husband that there will come a time when he's going to need Him most and he's going to say, "Lord, help me", and the Lord will laugh and say, "Lord, help me, and he will say, "Lord, heal me", and He will laugh and say, "Lord, Heal me". Because the Lord knows that his cry unto Him is only until he's delivered out of this trouble and that he has no desire to continue to cry to Him and that's why God will laugh and mock him, Proverbs 2. Lord, remind this husband that you give him plenty of warnings to live for you; plenty of opportunities to walk with you; and plenty of saints witnessing to him but he chooses to live his life his way. Lord, inform him that you don't like to be used and taken for granted just as we don't, but remind him that if we call upon you sincerely, that you will hear our cry. Lord, you said in your Word that if we do not have the spirit of Christ, we are none of yours, Romans 8:9b. Lord, remind this husband that you only hear the cries of the righteous, Psalm 34:17 and by learning this; we pray that he will become righteous today, In The Name of Jesus.

Chapter Six

THE UNGODLY MAN WITH A FAMILY

THE UNGODLY MAN WITH A FAMILY loves his family; he just doesn't make time to spend with them. He works, comes home, takes his seat in his favorite spot, with the remote, and will not move. He will give his check to his wife to handle the bills. If money is low, he wouldn't know, he doesn't check the books. If his wife is struggling, juggling the money to stretch it, he wouldn't know, he's asleep now. If the kids need to be disciplined, the wife is dad; if the kids need help with homework, the wife is the tutor; if the kids are hungry, the wife is the chef; if the house needs cleaning, the wife is the maid; all business calls, the wife handles; if the caller asks for Mr., she says, "This Is He". Whatever his children desire to have, it's okay with him. His wife can go any where she pleases, he doesn't mind and he won't check on her. She can spend money, he doesn't mind. She can take trips, he doesn't mind, he's not going, just she and the kids. When his wife wants to talk, he'll listen, he just won't respond. He will even watch movies with the family, remember, that's his hobby, sitting in his spot! He won't go to the movies. He is the nicest person in the world; just don't ask him to be a part of family functions. If gatherings are held at home, he'll be present, just in another area of the house. He makes no decisions, he has no suggestions, and they have no discussions. She's the Man!

If The Ungodly Man With A Family is asked, "Do you attend church?" He would answer, "My wife and kids attend, not me."

IT IS PRAYER TIME

Let us pray that this husband learns the Will, the Ways, the Works, and the Word of God. Let us pray that children receive guidance from both parents especially if both parents reside together. Let us pray that this husbands' mind is renewed and redirected so that he will understand and walk in his rightful position that God has given unto him as the head of his home. Let us pray that this husband is reminded that he is his children's example and they are learning from him. Let us pray that this husband walk circumspectly (with awareness) in the presence of his children. Let us pray that the way this husband handled matters prior to reading this book, are erased from the memory of his children so that they will take on their dad's new ways into their own households, In The Name of Jesus!

Chapter Seven

THE WICKED FAMILY MAN

THE WICKED FAMILY MAN is trying to understand what love is. He doesn't love himself; therefore, he can't love his wife. They are just married. He is controlling of everything and everyone in the household and abuses his authority. He participates in the kids' school activities, but he complains and fusses so much at the kids whereas the fun or joy is gone. He will attend the kids sporting events, but he yells at the child, embarrassing himself, his wife, and the child when an error is made. If the child scores, he's not excited about the child's accomplishment, he's excited about scoring. He is argumentative; it doesn't matter with whom or the location. He elevates his voice to show others that he's the head of his house. Whatever activity he and his family engage in, he is angry and bossy; he runs everything. He likes for his wife to look nice, but he is too stubborn to tell her that she does; however, if his wife is having a bad hair day, he will surely let it be known in a hurtful way. He makes promises to his family and doesn't keep them; though his family is hurt by the disappointments, it doesn't bother him. All of his plans are to hurt and destroy. You will find him in the church and working hard within the church. He will quickly volunteer assistance with the ministry, but his motive is to destroy, disrupt, or tear down. He does not have a heart to serve Jesus Christ but he makes others think that he does. The wicked, through the pride of his countenance, will not seek after God: God is not in all his thoughts, Psalm 10:4. He will go out of his way to buy gifts for people just so that he is loved by the recipients. The gift giving is to trick the recipients so that when his behavior is revealed to them, it isn't believed because he appears to be loving, kind, and a gracious giver. A wicked man taketh a gift out of the bosom to pervert the ways of judgment, Proverbs 17:23.

If The Wicked Family Man is asked, "What church do you attend?" He'd answer with his church name, the amount of years attended, and his titles. Remember, he attends church and is faithful, his motives are wicked.

IT IS PRAYER TIME!

Let us pray that this husband, the wicked family man be touched by the finger of God enabling him to come into the realness of Jesus Christ. Let us pray that his spirit is revealed to others so that they will know what to pray specifically. Let us pray that this husband is convicted by God of his deception. Let us pray that whomever this husband has come into contact with, that his spirit rests not on their shoulders and if it already has, we bind the spirit of lying, deception, greed, jealousy, envy, hatred, selfishness, pride, and all under cover spirits that rested upon or in the spirits of others and we loose the spirit of truth, righteousness, contentment, love, altruism, and benevolence, in the name of Jesus. Lord, comfort the wife and children and be their sustainer during this difficult time of their lives. Lord, show the wife how to live for You and what to instill into the lives of her children. Lord, teach her how to pray for her husband and kids; teach her how to recognize Your voice and to follow it. Lord, let her know that You hear all things; You created the ear, You see all things; You created the eye; You know all things; You created knowledge; and You can move any thing, You are in control. Lord, let this precious wife know that if You can control the seasons, the wind, the waves, the wild beasts, the growth of flowers, and all storms, then surely can You control the storms of her life. Lord, remind her that the sun shall come after the rain and that the rain won't last all day and just as the sun rises in the morning time, darkness shall go away. Lord, remind her that at the start of adversity, dark clouds form, but You Lord are in control and You shall end all storms! Lord, allow this family to rest under Your wings, In The Name of Jesus!

Chapter Eight

THE WICKED MAN WITH A FAMILY

THE WICKED MAN WITH A FAMILY loves his family in a way that no man can illustrate or envision. He may have a job, he may not; he may work a while when he gets a job, but then again, he may not; it depends upon how he feels; If he's educated and has a career, he'll work, but he's calling all shots. He pays all the bills and other folk bills too, if he chooses to; he doesn't have to consult his wife, he says that he's grown. He makes major purchases as he chooses; remember, he's grown; He shops freely and considers not "sales". He makes sure that his wardrobe is together, but considers not the wardrobe of his family's; he makes sure that his hair is cut regularly but his kids heads look like wigs; and will not offer money to them for haircuts. He is full of pride; he's selfish, and greedy of gain, He that is greedy of gain troubleth his own house, Proverbs 15:27. He that troubleth his own house shall inherit the wind, Proverbs 11:29. He's not a listener and has no interest in what's going on in his home. When he leaves the house in the a.m., and decides to return in the p.m., without speaking with his wife all day long, that's his business, you keep forgetting that he's grown. If he is a providing wicked husband with a family, he provides the "bare" necessities, nothing more. He is not under God's ruling, remember, he's wicked, oh I forgot, and grown. Is he likely to be abusive? Well, with no peace of mind, no Godly counsel, no prayer life, no thoughts of God, stressed out, miserable, mean, angry, tired, amongst other troubles, you answer that question! Remember, abuse can be physical, emotional, financial, sexual, verbal, and mental. He has no interest in the kids' school functions. He is unruly, distant and embarrassing; He looks for things to complain about just to punish the children. He does an excellent job at discouraging, raising his voice and threatening. He that is cruel troubleth his own flesh, Proverbs 11:17. The wife never knows what angers him because he's always angry. He's unloving, uncaring, and unconcerned about anything pertaining to the family or household. His poor ole' wife is just hanging in there waiting for a change.

If only this husband would realize that people love to hang around big spenders. He will go to dinner with groups of people and fight for the bill to pay it, but won't buy groceries for his own family; Many will intreat (plead) the favour of the prince (the ruler, the owner, the leader, the pastor, the head): and every man is a friend to him that giveth gifts, Proverbs 19:6. As long as he's spending, he'll always have so-called friends who loves him but when the money is short or when the well is dry; these friends are no longer thirsty. Remember, this husband is wicked; therefore, he may be engaged in liquid spirits and illegal substances. He doesn't mind his family attending church services or partaking in spiritual activities. He is one who has no interest in church and doesn't want to hear anything about church; and he has an attitude about it.

Let us pray that God remove this husbands' stony heart. Let us pray that God speaks a Word through us so that we can speak that very Word to wicked men to break up their heart of iron. For we know that God has the power to move mountains; He has the power to send down water from heaven in the form of morsels; He has the power to speak to wild animals and lead them to food; He has the power to speak to the waters and tell them to be still; He has the power to tell the waves in the water to be quiet; with His power, He spoke to a whale and told him to regurgitate; with His power, He turned the sea into dry land; with His power, He impregnated a barren woman; with His power, He gave a man a brand new hand; and with His power, He measures water in the hollow of His hand; God's yesterday's power is today's power and is tomorrow's power; He changes not; then surely can He transform a wicked mans' heart into a man of God's!

Chapter Nine

THE MAN WITH A FAMILY
Versus
THE FAMILY MAN

Below, view the thoughts and behavior of THE MAN WITH A FAMILY and THE FAMILY MAN. In the analogy, the Man With A Family and the Family Man are both Christians. To the men, if your behavior is found in the Family Man, thank God for His hand being upon you, your home, your family, and your life; however, if your behavior is found in the Man With A Family, repent, sincerely asking God to forgive you; ask God to assist you with the words to speak as you go to your wife and kids, to ask for forgiveness; cry out unto the Lord thanking Him for catching you, pulling you up out of deep waters, to enlighten you before sunset (death)! No one wants to miss out on Heaven; know that it is never too late to start over with God!

THE MAN WITH A FAMILY will take care of his family by paying the bills.

THE FAMILY MAN will take care of his family by being concerned about all of their needs. He is present; he listens with understanding, trains with patience, suggests with love, and assists with excitement.

THE MAN WITH A FAMILY wants the wife to know how he feels.

THE FAMILY MAN wants to know how his wife feels.

THE MAN WITH A FAMILY will take his family to church for prayer.

THE FAMILY MAN will take his family to God in prayer.

THE MAN WITH A FAMILY, when he feels good, he will take time to discuss problems and situations in circles, using psychology, calling it wisdom; using untruths, calling it discernment; and using threats and warnings, calling it head of household decisions.

THE FAMILY MAN will take time to discuss problems and situations, in details, with his wife until a mutual agreement is made.

THE MAN WITH A FAMILY most of the time is impatient; he yells concerning trivial matters; and he voids understanding.

THE FAMILY MAN talks to his wife and children.

THE MAN WITH A FAMILY loves when his family is away from the home.

THE FAMILY MAN loves to be around his family.

THE MAN WITH A FAMILY will call home to make sure that everyone and everything is in order before he arrives (there may be consequences).

THE FAMILY MAN will call home to make sure that everyone is home, safe or if they need him to bring something.

THE MAN WITH A FAMILY will make sure that he eats.

THE FAMILY MAN will make sure that everyone has eaten.

THE MAN WITH A FAMILY will retire for the evening while everyone is away from home, and he will not check on them.

THE FAMILY MAN will not retire for the evening unless everyone is home.

THE MAN WITH A FAMILY will retire for the evening not knowing if the kids are home. The doors and windows are wide open.

THE FAMILY MAN will not retire for the evening until his home is secured; all kids are asleep, all doors are locked, and all windows are shut.

THE MAN WITH A FAMILY withholds from his family (news, financial blessings, information, messages, etc.)

THE FAMILY MAN shares with his family.

THE MAN WITH A FAMILY assures his wife that he's going to handle situations; sharing with her no details or results.

THE FAMILY MAN assures his wife that he's going to handle situations; sharing with her details and results.

THE MAN WITH A FAMILY makes sure his wife is home.

THE FAMILY MAN makes sure his wife is happy.

THE MAN WITH A FAMILY impatiently waits in his bedroom (away from the kids) for the return of his wife; he has plans and he is stuck babysitting.

THE FAMILY MAN spends time with his kids and will not call it babysitting, he calls it bonding.

THE MAN WITH A FAMILY is excited when his wife enters the next room.

THE FAMILY MAN is excited when his wife enters the room.

THE MAN WITH A FAMILY makes plans.

THE FAMILY MAN makes plans with his family, for his family and will carry them out.

THE MAN WITH A FAMILY hears his family.

THE FAMILY MAN listens to his family.

THE MAN WITH A FAMILY offends his family.

THE FAMILY MAN defends his wife and children.

THE MAN WITH A FAMILY prays with others and for others.

THE FAMILY MAN prays with his wife and kids and he prays for them.

THE MAN WITH A FAMILY voice carries throughout the house the aroma of anger, strife, hatred, and war.

THE FAMILY MAN voice carries throughout the house the beautiful fragrances of love, excitement, peace, and joy.

THE MAN WITH A FAMILY discourages his wife and kids.

THE FAMILY MAN encourages his wife and kids.

THE MAN WITH A FAMILY calls his house a home.

THE FAMILY MAN makes his house a home.

THE MAN WITH A FAMILY makes sure his wife knows that it's her job to have plenty of food in the home.

THE FAMILY MAN assures that there is plenty of food in the home.

THE MAN WITH A FAMILY has an interest in his whereabouts daily.

THE FAMILY MAN has an interest in the whereabouts of his family daily.

THE MAN WITH A FAMILY is irrational; he has no interest in the thoughts, feelings, or concerns of his family.

THE FAMILY MAN is rational; his family is his main concern each day.

THE MAN WITH A FAMILY with live-in step children learns to "signify" the step children and publish with a soft voice that there are partialities.

THE FAMILY MAN with live-in step children learns to "unify" the family and publish with a loud voice that there will be no partialities.

THE MAN WITH A FAMILY with live-in step children makes sure that all of "**his**" kids' needs are met.

THE FAMILY MAN with live-in step children makes sure that all of "**the**" kids' needs are met.

THE MAN WITH A FAMILY with live-in step children speaks nicely to "**his**" children.

THE FAMILY MAN with live-in step children speaks nicely to all of "**the**" children.

THE MAN WITH A FAMILY with live-in step children assures all of the children that he is the head of the house and he will decide if his wife has been disrespected or not (if his child disrespects her, it's a misunderstanding; if her child disrespects her, it's punishment). Remember, he decides!

THE FAMILY MAN with live-in step children assures all of the children that his wife will not be disrespected in any manner.

THE MAN WITH A FAMILY works hard so it looks as if he's comforting his family.

THE FAMILY MAN works hard to comfort his family.

THE MAN WITH A FAMILY is open with his wife; keeping secrets when purchasing, making decisions, and disciplining the children; however, he assures her that as long as he is taking care of home, she ought to be satisfied.

THE FAMILY MAN is open with his wife, keeping no secrets when purchasing, making decisions, and disciplining the children.

THE MAN WITH A FAMILY makes time for others.

THE FAMILY MAN makes time for his family.

THE MAN WITH A FAMILY listens to ungodly, inexperienced, personal and professional counselors, magazines, statistics, media news, and the internet for instructions to run his household.

THE FAMILY MAN listens to God and Godly counsel for instructions to run his household.

THE MAN WITH A FAMILY will not abuse his wife (in his eyesight); he calls it being the HEAD of the house; he says what he wants, how he wants, when he wants; when she is hurt, he blames her for his actions and his reactions; he's never at fault.

THE FAMILY MAN will not abuse his wife in
any way (emotionally, physically, or verbally); he knows that God ordained him to cherish and nourish her.

THE MAN WITH A FAMILY assures his children that his wife has a voice.

THE FAMILY MAN assures his children that his wife has a voice and it shall be heard!

THE MAN WITH A FAMILY degrades his wife in the presence of his children and others.

THE FAMILY MAN praises his wife in the presence of his children and others.

THE MAN WITH A FAMILY has open hands, always dispensing money to others, just because, never having anything extra for his wife.

THE FAMILY MAN has open hands, always dispensing money to his wife just because and just for her.

THE MAN WITH A FAMILY knows that whatever his wife has, he has, but if she has more, it diminishes his power or control. Therefore, he holds her back in ministry, education, or profession.

THE FAMILY MAN knows that whatever his wife has, he has. Therefore, he encourages her to move forward in ministry, education, or profession.

THE MAN WITH A FAMILY knows and understands the benefits of honoring his wife, but he does not believe. However, he does believe that she is weak.

THE FAMILY MAN knows and understands the benefits of honoring his wife (Likewise, ye husbands, dwell with them according to knowledge, giving honour unto the wife, as unto the weaker vessel, and as being heirs together of the grace of life; that your prayers be not hindered I Peter 3:7). He believes the Word, stands on the Word, and knows that she's not weak because he gains strength from her.

THE MAN WITH A FAMILY knows that **because of him**, his wife is as a fruitful vine by the sides of his house and **because of him**, his children are like olive plants around **his** dinner table.

THE FAMILY MAN knows that **because of God**, his wife is as a fruitful vine by the sides of his house and **because of God**, his children are like olive plants around the dinner table (Thy wife shall be as a fruitful vine by the sides of thine house: thy children like olive plants round about thy table, Psalm 128:3).

THE MAN WITH A FAMILY tells his family that they ought to praise and thank God for him.

THE FAMILY MAN praises and thanks God daily for his family.

THE MAN WITH A FAMILY knows that he found a wife, though he wasn't looking for one, and he knows that he found a good thing. However, his wife will never know this and neither will others; he is afraid that light or attention will shine upon her and this would diffuse his light, in his eyesight.

THE FAMILY MAN knows that because he found a wife, he found a good thing (Whoso findeth a wife findeth a good thing, and obtaineth favour of the LORD, Proverbs, 18:22).

Chapter Ten

THE LEADER

Man that is in honour, and understandeth not, is like the beasts that perish, Psalm 49:20.

A husband, pastor, principal, teacher, father, president, supervisor, chief, manager, mayor, colonel, or anyone with subordinates who dictates, directs, decides, and delegates, is a MAN IN HONOR.

This man in honor, our leader, who understands not, is like the beasts that perish! There are some things that this man in honor must understand. **WHAT MUST HE UNDERSTAND?**

HE MUST UNDERSTAND that he is not greater than God.

HE MUST UNDERSTAND that regardless to titles, positions, gender, race, education, or salaries, Jesus is the Most High God.

HE MUST UNDERSTAND that priorities must be set; God, home, job.

HE MUST UNDERSTAND that a man in honor is one who honors his wife.

HE MUST UNDERSTAND that their children will not always be children and if time is spent with them when they're young, time will be spent with him when he ages.

HE MUST UNDERSTAND that a man in honor is one who honors God first, not himself.

HE MUST UNDERSTAND that God is no respecter of persons; His Word stands for everyone, not just others; what so ever a man soweth, that shall he also reapeth.

HE MUST UNDERSTAND that when he is placed in a position to have rule over others, he is in the position to sprinkle salt on others. We are the salt in the world; salt is seasoning that enhances tastelessness.

HE MUST UNDERSTAND that when a man in honor enters a room, the light of the Lord should shine upon him. When he speaks, his speech should be seasoned with salt.

HE MUST UNDERSTAND that when a man in honor exits a room, the sweet-smelling savor should continue to linger and all in attendance ought to have a taste of Jesus, desiring more.

HE MUST UNDERSTAND that because he is in his big chair, sitting upon his great throne means little to God. However, if he is living the life of Jesus Christ, abiding by His statutes, commandments, and laws in the Bible, then he is considered an asset unto the Kingdom. As he sits in his big chair, the light of the Lord ought to be shining upon him; always exemplifying Jesus Christ around his wife, children, family, friends, and strangers.

HE MUST UNDERSTAND that when he speaks, he's representing Jesus Christ.

A Man In Honor who understands not, is like a beast who perishes. What is it that this man in honor **UNDERSTANDS NOT?**

HE UNDERSTANDS NOT that he is caught up in his title, position, and authority. (Refer to my book Humbling Thyself)

HE UNDERSTANDS NOT that whatsoever goes up, must come down, one way or another. (Refer to my book Humbling Thyself)

HE UNDERSTANDS NOT that his throne is short lived.

HE UNDERSTANDS NOT that one day he, himself, must perish.

HE UNDERSTANDS NOT that we have brought nothing into this world and it is certain that we will carry nothing out.

HE UNDERSTANDS NOT that his position is a test.

    a. To see if he will follow or continue to follow Jesus.

    b. To see if he is going to lead others to follow or continue to follow Jesus.

HE UNDERSTANDS NOT that if he does not follow Christ, he is headed for destruction, maybe not in life, but in death.

HE UNDERSTANDS NOT that if he does not lead others to Christ, and he has the power to do it, he shall suffer, maybe not in life, but in death.

HE UNDERSTANDS NOT that a man who voids understanding, striketh with the hands.

HE UNDERSTANDS NOT that it is wisdom that he lacks; he uses his weapon of power against the weak. The weapon used may be abuse of any kind; promotion withholdings, demotions, layoffs, deception.

HE UNDERSTANDS NOT that all he needs is wisdom of God to equip him with decision making, training, listening, guiding, and more.

HE UNDERSTANDS NOT that a man lacking wisdom moves according to his abilities, knowledge, viewpoints, or perspectives.

"THE BEASTS THAT PERISH"

Man that is in honour, and understandeth not, is like the **beasts that perish**, Psalm 49:20.

A dead lion in the street is good for nothing; this is the same as a man that is in honor and understands not.

A tree that produces corrupt fruit is good for nothing but to be hewn down and cast into the fire.

We are to be as a tree planted by the waters, and that spreadeth out her roots by the river, and shall not see when heat cometh, but her leaf shall be green; (when trials, tribulation, persecution, trouble, adversity of any kind comes, we shall not see it because we are so full of God's sap that when it appears, that's when we're faced with it, and that's when we deal with it. Because we have been prepared with strength, the Word, stored up prayers, and advanced praise, we can better handle situations; and because of our preparation, we shall not pass out when we hear shocking news, we will not lose our minds or have sudden heart attacks behind the news; this is what "her leaf shall be green" means. Though we're faced with a dilemma, the sap of God is still flowing); **and shall not be careful in the year of drought, neither shall cease from yielding fruit, Jeremiah 17:8**. This means that because we have made the Lord our hope and all of our trust and faith is in Him, when a drought comes; when layoffs come; when furloughs come; when downsizing comes; when company close-ups come; when repossession comes; when a spouse just "speaks of separation" comes; when strikes come; when the account is low; when the closet is bare; we don't have to worry, we don't have to be watchful, we don't have to be careful; all we have to be is trustful and prayerful! The promise is "we shall not cease from yielding (producing) fruit. Stand on it!

Therefore, to be like this tree that is full of moisture requires work. Though the tree just sits still and intake the water by the river, it seems pretty simple for us to do. The tree is standing, but through many types of storms (hail, snow, thunder, wind, tornadoes, and hurricanes), it is anchored to Jesus, He is the water; He is the strength.

In order for our tree to have a continuous flow of sap we must pray, fast, praise, worship, meditate, and consecrate always. We also must hear the Word of God, Believe the Word of God, study the Word of God, live the Word of God, spread the Word of God, live uprightly before the Lord, walk in righteousness, worketh righteousness, speak the truth, love Jesus, pray for others, visit the sick and shut-in, help one another, have compassion for others, bear one another's burdens, love your wife, take care of your family and there's much more, but this is a start!

MEN IN HONOR!

Oh Men in Honor, are you full of knowledge of God or are you just full of knowledge?

Oh Men in Honor, are you full of knowledge of God and spreading it or are you just full of knowledge of God?

Oh Men in Honor, understand that you are to be that tree, full of sap, leading people to the sap; and when you perish, it shall be known by many that your death was precious because your death was in Christ. Precious in the sight of the LORD is the death of His saints, Psalm 116:15!

Oh Men in Honor, in all of your standing; whatever you're standing for; whatever you're standing against; whatever you're standing upon; whatever you're standing by; whatever you're standing in; whatever you're standing through, if you are not standing on the promises of God and if you're not standing on God's Word, you're standing on your own strength; how great is your strength and how long will the greatness of your strength be?

Oh Men in Honor Take a Stand

Oh Men in Honor Take a Bow!

Oh Men in Honor, we thank God for you and your accomplishments. It must be made known that your work will be greater when you work for the Lord. In everything we do, we must honor the Lord and ask Him for direction in doing it, then thank Him for it. (Refer to my book Humbling Thyself).

If all of our direction is coming from the Lord, even if it's through others, and we abide by it, we are already working for the Lord and if we are working for the Lord, then our work shall not be in vain. Also, whatever we do for the Lord is greater than doing a work for any man. Though we may not be the proprietor of the company that we are employed by, we still must do a work as if we are working for the Lord only.

If we do this, then we will enjoy what we do. Oh Men in Honor, if you do not have a relationship with Jesus, know today that you can develop one. If you're not a Christian, know that you can become one today! Learn how to become saved below. This is our three-step Plan of Salvation.

Chapter Eleven

THREE STEPS TO THE PLAN OF SALVATION!

Then Peter said unto them, **Repent**, and **be baptized** every one of you in the name of Jesus Christ for the remission of sins, and ye shall **receive the gift of the Holy Ghost**. For the promise is unto you, and to your children, and to all that are afar off, even as many as the Lord our God shall call, Acts 2:38-39.

Being a Christian is living the life of Jesus Christ by first **dying** (repenting, killing sin), being **buried** (baptized, burying sin), and **resurrecting** (receiving the Holy Ghost, set free from sin, rising to new life). Follow the ways, the works, the will, and the Word of Jesus Christ; this makes you a Christian, living a Christ-like life.

Act upon the following steps!

STEP ONE: REPENTANCE

Jesus said in His Word that if we drink of His water, we shall never thirst again. When we drink of His water, we shall continuously be full of His sap, never running dry. The drinking of His water is repentance, telling God how sorry we are for sinning, for not living according to His Word; for not treating our children according to His ways; for not treating our wives according to the Bible; for not learning about Him; for not thinking about Him; and for not directing our family to Jesus. Repentance means that we have a change of mind; a change of heart; and a new understanding. That change of mind is to be more like Jesus Christ. That change of heart is to have the desire to do the will of God and no longer having the desire to do "our" own will.

When we have the desire to do the will of God, God will show us His Will, John 7:17. That new understanding is realizing that we cannot make it in life without God and that we must "seek" His face on earth in order for us to "see" His face in Heaven.

So, the result of true repentance is turning completely away from an ungodly lifestyle to a Godly lifestyle.

We're not speaking of repentance of ungodly acts, sins, or behavior that we sometimes engage in as Christians, but we're speaking of turning our lives over to God, asking His forgiveness for "all" of our sins; converting our lives from ungodliness to righteousness; being delivered out of the power of darkness, translated into the Kingdom of Jesus Christ.

When we no longer engage in ungodly acts; having no desire to do these acts again; and in actuality, never do these acts again; we have not repented. We have just turned away from that which was ungodly.

Example: If you have given up alcohol drinking, you've just stopped cold turkey, years have passed and you have not again returned to alcohol, you have not repented. All you have done was stopped drinking or turned away from drinking. The same goes for gambling, lying, stealing, etc.

So, because you have turned away from ungodliness (alcoholism, drugs, fornication, etc.), without the mind to turn to Godliness, you have not repented, though the
decision you made was good; don't start back.

True repentance involves the change of heart, the change of mind, a new understanding and a change of activity; walking in the light and continuously living for Jesus Christ. Remember, **the Lord will open your eyes, and turn you from darkness to light, and from the power of Satan unto Him, that you may receive forgiveness of sins, and inheritance among them which are sanctified by faith that is in Him, Acts 26:18.**

And they shall teach no more every man his neighbour, and every man his brother, saying, Know the LORD: for they shall all know me, from the least of them unto the greatest of them, saith the LORD: for **I will forgive their iniquity**, and **I will remember their sin no more**, **Jeremiah 31:34**.

If my people, which are called by my name, shall humble themselves, and pray, and seek my face, and **turn from their wicked ways**; then will I hear from heaven, **and will forgive their sin**, and will heal their land, **II Chronicles 7:14.** If we confess our sins, he is faithful and just to **forgive us our sins**, and to cleanse us from all unrighteousness, **I John 1:9.**

STEP TWO: WATER BAPTISM

Water baptism in the name of Jesus, by immersion, is an open expression demonstrating to the world that you have repented of your sins. Also, baptism is the first command to obey after repentance. When you are immersed into the water, your sins are actually buried and you are washed clean by the blood of Jesus. The water symbolizes the blood of Jesus; His blood is pure. When you are lifted from the water, you are a new creature; you are born again, born of the water. So actually, you go down into the water a sinner, but you rise up a saint!

Step Three: Receiving The Holy Ghost

The Holy Ghost or Holy Spirit is a gift from God. The evidence of receiving it is that you speak in a different language, unknown to you and unlearned by you; or speaking in other tongues. The Spirit of the Lord gives the utterance, you utilize your vocal cords, but God gives the tongues. To be baptized in the Holy Ghost or Holy Spirit or born of the Spirit is the same as receiving the Holy Ghost.

The wind bloweth where it listeth, and thou hearest the sound thereof, but canst not tell whence it cometh, and whither it goeth, so is everyone that is born of the Spirit, John 3:8.

This verse means that in order for us to be born of the Spirit, there must be evidence. That evidence is a sound heard by us just as there is a sound heard when the wind blows. The sound that we hear as evidence of being born of the Spirit is speaking in other tongues as the Spirit gives utterance, Acts 2:1-4.

The "sound" Jesus speaks of in John 3:8 is the "other tongues" that's described in Acts 2:4. Acts 2:9-11 displays the many languages spoken by the Jews out of every nation under heaven. Listening to the sounds of the various languages better describes the sound Jesus speaks of in John 3:8.

Who, when they come down, prayed for them, that they might receive the Holy Ghost. (For as yet he was fallen upon none of them: only they were baptized in the name of the Lord Jesus.). Then laid they their hands on them,
and they received the Holy Ghost, Acts 8:15-17.

These verses mean that Peter and John were called on to preach the word in Samaria. The Samaritans were baptized with water but they did not receive the Holy Ghost until the apostles laid their hands upon them after first praying. Acts 8:18, Simon witnessed the tongue speaking and the power and in amazement, he wanted the Holy Ghost as well. He offered money for this great empowerment.

Some believe that once an individual repents, and is immersed in water, that they have received the Holy Ghost automatically after their baptism. If this is true, then what was it that Simon witnessed and felt intensely that he was willing to pay to possess?

While Peter yet spake these words, the Holy Ghost fell on all them which heard the word. And they of the circumcision which believed were astonished, as many as come with Peter, because that on the Gentiles also was poured out the gift of the Holy Ghost. For they heard them speak with tongues, and magnify God, Acts 10:44-46.

These verses mean that while Peter was preaching about believing in Jesus, whosoever believed would receive remission of sins (forgiveness of sins) and the Holy Ghost fell on all who were listening. The gift of the Holy Ghost was poured out on all who were with Peter and they spoke with tongues and magnified God.

And as I began to speak, the Holy Ghost fell on them, as on us at the beginning. Then remembered I, the word of the Lord, how that he said, John indeed baptized with water; but ye shall be baptized with the Holy Ghost,
Acts 11:15-16.

These verses mean that Peter again was preaching and the Holy Ghost fell on them just as it did in Acts 2:4. Peter then remembered words spoken by the Lord that not only are we to be baptized with water, but also with the Holy Ghost.

Romans 8:9-11 – But ye are not in the flesh, but in the Spirit, **if** so be that the Spirit of God dwell in you. Now **if** any man have not the Spirit of Christ, he is none of His. But **if** Christ be in you, the body is dead because of sin; but the Spirit is life because of righteousness. But **if** the Spirit of him that raised up Jesus from the dead dwell in you, he that raised up Christ from the dead shall also quicken your mortal bodies by his Spirit that dwelleth in you.

The verses above mean that the spirit of Jesus does not dwell within every one. Pay close attention to; "**if**, **if so**, **if any man**, **if Christ be in you**, **if the Spirit**." The Holy Ghost is power! The power that raised Jesus from the dead is the same power that lives inside of the Holy Ghost filled person. This power is greater than the power that husbands have over wives. This power is greater than the power shepherds have over sheep; this power is greater than the power presidents have over countries; principals over schools; or parents over children. Leaders, great power is not controlling the minds of people. Great power is controlling your group, institute, church, establishment, or union with the power of God "the Holy Ghost. When you speak, the people, your subordinates, will move because of the power that is within you and the power that is upon you. They will do whatever it is that you need them to do without questions, hassles, or complaints. The Holy Ghost will teach you how to run your business, it will strengthen your business, and it will warn you of trouble. Just think leaders, what if everyone in your office or company was Holy Ghost filled or all of the leaders under you were Holy Ghost filled, that would be great power!

The Holy Ghost power keeps us from sinning or it deters us from sinning!

We must be born again of the water and of the Spirit!

Be Blessed!

Chapter Twelve
A NOTE TO THE WOMEN

My prayer is that your prayer life increases greatly upon reading my book. If you have been blessed to have a God-fearing husband, who God-rears the children, and God-spears the household, be grateful unto God and unto your husband, praise God and praise your husband!

Pray for all of the women who are awaiting healing and deliverance from God with their spiritual lives, marital lives, and family lives.

Pray for all Christian husbands, including yours, so that they will continue to walk in holiness.

Pray for the ungodly and wicked husbands asking God to drop a Word in their spirit to redirect them.

Pray for all hurting wives and children who cannot express to anyone their family troubles. Ask God to comfort, protect, and bless them.

Ask God to give the wives the words to say to encourage their husbands to live holy lives.

Ask God to reveal or expose the unrighteousness of husbands to the "husbands" and to others who would never believe his acts of conduct. After exposure, ask God to convict him, cause shame to overshadow him and unction him to repent in the name of Jesus.

Ask God to remind them that He sees everything, He hears everything, and He knows everything. Ask God to remind them that it will not rain always, the sun shall
shine. Ask God to remind them that He is their help and though they can't speak **up** or **out**, just continue to speak **to** Jesus Christ.

Intercede in prayer for the absent fathers who have a desire to be present in their children's lives, but are blocked for whatever reasons. Children need both parents even if step-parents are present. There's nothing greater than a man teaching his son, by example, how to be a man or a man teaching his daughter, by example, how she's to be treated by a man.

Ask God to speak to the wife who has difficulty reverencing her husband because of his inappropriate behavior. Ask God to remind her that He gives us a choice, here on earth, as to where we want to spend eternity and if Heaven is our choice, He has written instructions for us to follow which are in the Bible. If we do not follow His instructions, we won't make it in. We must reverence our husbands in spite of circumstances.

Ladies, we must reverence our husbands, Ephesians 5:33!

Ask God to strengthen her in His Word so that she's able to abide by His Word at all times, especially during hard times.

To the aspiring wives, when you pray, ask God to bless you with **your own** husband, then ask Him to show you **your** husband. Next, ask God to prepare you to be the wife you need to be for **your** husband. Then, thank and praise God for **your** husband before you meet him. When God shows you **your** husband, you will know him because God will reveal it to **your** spirit.

THE MILK CARTON

During meditation a few years ago, the Lord spoke to me and said, "Handle prayer just as you handle a milk carton." The Lord knew I did not fully understand so He said, "What do you do with your empty milk carton?" I said, "Put it in the kitchen trash can." The Lord said, "Then where does it go?" I said, "Outside to the dumpster." Then the Lord said, "Then where does it go?" I said, "Where ever the trash men take it." Then the Lord said, "Then where does it go?" I said, "I don't know." Then He said "Do you worry about it?" I said, "No." He said, "Do you think about it?" I said, "No." He said, "What do you do about the carton?" I said, "Nothing." He said, "Do you go get more milk?" I said, "Yes." The Lord said, "When it's empty, what do you do with the empty carton." I said, "I throw it away." He said, "Then where does it go." The Lord had me to repeat this process aloud three or four times to be sure I handle my prayers in the same manner. To the intercessors, this means we do not have to repeat prayers. God created the ear; He can hear us once. This means after we pray, worry no more. This means to petition God for something else or present a new prayer request just as we purchase new cartons of milk. When the carton is placed in the trash can, it is no longer yours.

You don't have to worry about the expiration date or the temperature of the milk any longer, it's gone. Same with prayer, the matter is no longer yours. As we put the empty milk carton in the hands of the "can", we must put our prayers in the hands of "the Son of Man." Jesus!

AFTERWORD

Thank you so much for spreading the message in this book throughout the world. Because of you and your support, husbands, wives, and families are changed. As the "husbands" walk more in righteousness, the body will follow and that's unity. You have been a blessing to me and I pray that I have been a blessing to you.

Love,

Brenda B. Matthews

www.ingramcontent.com/pod-product-compliance
Lightning Source LLC
Chambersburg PA
CBHW031421040426
42444CB00005B/666